ΙU

THE KINGFISHER'S SOUL

ROBERT ADAMSON was born in Sydney in 1943 and grew up in Neutral Bay and on the Hawkesbury River, New South Wales. From 1970 to 1985 he edited Australia's *New Poetry* magazine, and in 1988, with Juno Gemes, he established Paper Bark Press, one of Australia's leading poetry publishers. His many award-winning publications include an autobiography, *Inside Out* (2004), two books of autobiographical fiction, and nearly 20 books of poetry, including *Reading the River: Selected Poems* (2004) and *The Kingfisher's Soul* (2009) from Bloodaxe.

ROBERT ADAMSON

THE
Kingfisher's
Soul

BLOODAXE BOOKS

ISBN: 978 1 85224 820 8

First published 2009 by
Bloodaxe Books Ltd,
Highgreen,
Tarset,
Northumberland NE48 1RP.

www.bloodaxebooks.com
For further information about Bloodaxe titles
please visit our website or write to
the above address for a catalogue.

Bloodaxe Books Ltd acknowledges
the financial assistance of
Arts Council England, North East.

This project has been assisted by the Australian Government through
the Australia Council for the Arts, its arts funding and advisory body.

Cover design: Neil Astley & Pamela Robertson-Pearce.

Printed in Great Britain by Bell & Bain Limited, Glasgow, Scotland.

for Juno, always

ACKNOWLEDGEMENTS

Some of these poems are reprinted from *Reading the River: Selected Poems* (Bloodaxe Books, 2004) and *The Goldfinches of Baghdad* (Flood Editions, USA, 2006). The poems in part three were written between 2006 and 2008.

Robert Adamson would like to acknowledge the generous support of the Literature Board of the Australia Council during the composition of this book.

Grateful acknowledgement is also made to the editors and publishers of magazines, newspapers and anthologies in which some of new poems appeared: *ABR*, *The Age*, *The Australian*, *The Australian Book Review*, *The Australian's ALR*, *The Best Australian Poems 2006*, *The Best Australian Poems 2007*, *The Best Australian Poetry 2006*, *The Best Australian Poetry 2007*, *The Best Australian Poetry 2008*, *Chicago Review*, *Heat*, *Jacket 34 online* and *The Weekend Australian Magazine*.

CONTENTS

PART ONE

Walking by the River

He walked waist-deep
through his thoughts,
emotions, a tangle of vines
and tree-creepers.

His words were finches,
flying before him
as he swung his arms –
scrambled paragraphs.

A waterfall sounded
ahead of his walk,
chipped words cracked
with each step. He came to

a calm place, opulent phrases
in bloom: purple-fruited
pigface, the blackthorn's
blue-black sloe.

Ungaretti at Broken Bay

A blue heron, foraging for its young,
circles a stranded cicada – then
stops, assuming a position of aim.
A family of redhead finches
pour out from a hole in a hollow
tree stump of yellowbox.
Cats scavenge for fish heads
by the cleaning slab; water rats
nest under sun-bleached planks
that jut from a mudbank.
The tide's right and Giuseppe
prepares to set his long lines –
He throws out the kellick:
when it takes a grip on the bottom
the traces will follow, with their
butterflied fillets of mullet,
pinned to hollow-point 5.0 hooks –
these baits, still seeping blood,
will flutter through the water column.

A Bend in the Euphrates

In a dream on a sheet of paper I saw
a pencil drawing of lovers: they seemed perfect,

Adam and Eve possibly. Stepping into reality,
I read lines of a poem on a piece

of crumpled rag I kept trying to smooth – Egyptian
linen, so fine it puzzled to imagine such a delicate

loom. In a flash I saw two dirty-breasted ibis
and heard their heads swish: black bills

swiped the cloudy stream, and in the rushes
I heard needles stitching, weaving features

into the landscape, clacking as they shaped
an orange tree, then switched a beat to invent

blue-black feathers for crows, the pointed
wedges of their beaks. A fox rustles

through wild lantana as I step through into
the garden and, becoming part of the weave,

notice the tide turn, its weight eroding mudbanks,
bringing filth in from the ocean. A raft of flotsam

breaks away, a duckling perched on the thicket
of its hump. I use the murky river for my ink,

draw bearings on the piece of cloth, sketch
a pair of cattle egrets bullying teal into flight.

The map's folded away, I travel by heart now,
old lessons are useless. I shelter from bad weather

in the oyster farmer's shack. The moon falls in a
column of light, a glowing epicycle –

this pale wandering spot on my writing table
these fragments of regret:

The Kingfisher's Soul

(for Juno)

A wave hits the shoreline of broken boulders,
explodes, fans into fine spray, a fluid wing
then drops back onto the tide: A spume
of arterial blood. Our eyes can be gulled by what
the brain takes in – our spirits take flight
each time we catch sight out – feathers of smoke
dissolve in air as we glide towards clarity.

In the old days I used to think art
that was purely imagined could fly higher
than anything real. Now I feel a small fluttering
bird in my own pulse, a connection to sky.
Back then a part of me was only half alive:
your breath blew a thicket of smoke from my eyes
and brought that half to life. There's no

evidence, nothing tangible, and no philosopher
of blood considering possibilities,
weighing up feathers, or souls. One day
some evidence could spring from shadows
as my body did in rejecting the delicious poisons,
the lure of dark song. You came with a wind
in your gaze, flinging away trouble's screw,

laughing at the King of Hell's weird command;
you created birthdays and the cheekbones
of family – I was up, gliding through life
and my fabrications, thought's soft cradle.
I scoured memory's tricks from my *own* memory,
its shots and score cards, those ambiguous lyrics –
Clear bird song was not human-song, hearing became

nets and shadowy vibrations, the purring
air, full of whispers and lies. I felt blank pages,
indentations created by images, getting by
with the shapes I made from crafted habits.
You taught me how to weigh the harvest of light.
There was bright innocence in your spelling,
I learned to read again through wounded eyes.

Wispy spiders of withdrawal sparked with static
electricity across skin, tiny veins, a tracery of
coppery wires, conducting pain to nerve
patterns: all lightweights, to your blood's iron.
You brought along new light to live in
as well as read with – before you came, whenever
I caught a glimpse of my own blood, it seemed

a waterfall of bright cells as it bled away.
Clouds of euphony, created by its loss, became
holes in thinking, pretend escape hatches. You're now
a rush, wings through the channels of my coronary
arteries. We slept together when you conjured
a bed in your Paddington tree-house: barbless hours,
peace appeared and said: *Soon*, the future awaits you.

I stepped into the day, by following your gaze.

The Whitebait

The first winter frost
burns delicate leaves
of basil in terracotta pots,

coats the kangaroo-paw
ferns; white fur collars
on crimson buds.

The hardy starlings
flit about, pecking dirt;
singing, click, click.

I read the morning news
and then think of
the unblinking eyes

of silver gulls –
their beaks slash at
whitebait still kicking

in plastic boxes on the wharf
of the Fisherman's Co-op.

In our garden, a patch
of sunlight moves across
the grass, eating the crystals of ice.

Brush Turkey in the Cold Room

(for Anthony Lawrence)

At the Fisherman's Co-op
I stand in the cold room and look out the window's
scale-plastered-glass, the river's being
whipped up by a westerly, chop cuts across
the ferry's prow and brakes into white spray.

Someone's hung a no smoking sign in the freezer.
We puffed our way through the best days of our lives,
and shortness of breath didn't bother us.

Dutch walks up from the pontoon with a box
of dusky flathead, the neon light from the hood
of the freezer flares all around his hair –
He's a classic cast the net on the other side
sort of bloke – he shovels flakes of ice
onto his catch, then lights up a rollie, at 50
he's still strong as a White Ox – 'We spend our life
waiting – lines, fish, love and money and in no order,
whatever comes up first' – he repeats every time he drinks.

A brush turkey walks into the cold room,
glances sideways, and stupidly, senses no danger –
Dutch keeps shovelling ice – its tail a black fan
vertically held, its wattle bright as orange anti-fouling paint.

My Grandfather's Ice Pigeons

My grandfather would walk into the house,
on a summer evening after his work, then empty
his catch of mud crabs into the bath-tub;
they'd flow out in a stream of ice-flurry from
his four-gallon drums, then settle in a heap of
black and olive speckled claws, spiky legs
and back flappers waving frantically. One night
my mother caught me holding a broomstick
with an angry claw clamped around it.
She ordered me to stay away from the crabs
reminding me why Uncle Eric lost his finger;
they could snap a clothes prop in two.
My mother went back to the city. I stayed
a week and my grandmother showed me
what to do, first throw one into a bucket of ice
to slow it down, then bind the claws together
with kingfisher-blue twine in a slip knot.
Old Dutch would come to take them
to the Co-op in his truck, packed into fish boxes
covered with ice. My grandfather would leave
again for his next catch, he'd take some pigeons
with him in a cage on his trawler. If he
had a good haul, he'd let one of the birds go,
when it came home it was my job to ride my bike
into town to order the ice. When I reached
the Co-op, Dutch would ask how many pigeons?
If more than one, it was a box of ice a bird.
He'd send the ice to my grandfather next morning
on the mail boat. They talk about the time
Fa Fa got drunk up the river at Spencer,
the river postman saw him through the mist
one morning, balancing on net-boards at the stern
of his boat, singing aloud, throwing pigeons at the sky.

The Lakeside Rituals

Drive through the town, don't stop
at the hotel, pass the marlin with its neon sword,
notice the pelicans perched
on the streetlights, pull up and park
by the lake. It's the dark of the moon
and the bulrushes smell of burning kerosene.

Men wade through lake water,
they follow children who lead the way
with flaming wicks, they are scoop-netting prawns.
They arrived with their families
in cars and trucks, some bring tents.
Behind drawn blinds in the caravan park

husbands get drunk or slip away.
When the last group comes in with their catch,
fires glow in red-hot drums –
they boil buckets of salt water
and play country music or rock.
They do a kind of dance, not really dancing,

attending to rituals, sometimes
a fist-fight will break out, or even a stabbing
may happen. It's mainly a double-shuffle
and a song. Then they feast on the catch –
peeling prawns and drinking beer,
making toast or boiling billies as the curlews call.

Narkissos on a Gamefishing Boat

The surface of the river
caught by an eddy
and the clipping
wing of a westerly wind

crazed mirrors
in every leaping wave
reflecting cubist
faces on each edge

the water lapping
on the side of the boat
hissing and coughing
catbird songs

at the river's mouth
where sweet water
meets the salt
tide's lapping tongue

I listen to echoes
in the hull as the V8
thrums drunk on petrol
fumes and calling

for more dark music
the sunlight shatters
reflections and the white
foam of the wave hits home

The Net

(after Attila József)

Curly hair's thinning, dry flakes
drift around my shoulders –
I've lost my fountain pen again.
Uncle Eric, the family's last professional
fisherman, is dead. Don't worry
though, I'm not alone.

I trawl my bloodstream
and nerves, my genetic fishing net,
in these dark waters
catch a few sparks of light –
my mesh's torn, so I hang it up
and grab a needle.

Now my net's hung out
on the clothes line, I can see
translucent scales, white twigs
from swayback river gums; twisted knots
of hair from ribbonfish tails,
stars in a firmament.

The Fledglings

They came ashore, human dregs from the ferry,
some of the men hauling cages on long poles.
The imprisoned calls of birds caught in wakes
of air at the back of the smugglers' heads.

Then they moved along the avenue and passed
before the window; I sat in my workshop
cutting patches of cloth that no longer held
the wind – to be used as flags on fishing boats –

They came each afternoon, trudged
over the cobblestones, their heels clicking
as the first koels of summer made their piercing calls.
Night held the promise of white asparagus

on the shore, iron-rich seaweed at the mouth
of the bay. On dark nights I longed to converse
about the brain-fever birds – there was no interest
until you came, with your ear for

the right nuance as it vibrated across
acoustic threads of talk. These words seek
the delicate vessel once called the soul,
so take care my love, or they may stitch one – *flag-like* –

to the back of your head. These birds
so highly audible by day, are rarely seen – who bears
witness to their dark migrations? They arrive in time
for spring, constantly raiding the nests of others.

When brain-fever birds perch, they become
flowering branches in jacarandas – they sing their
two notes and lay soft eggs within thoughts
that fledge inside our heads, as a longing for flight.

In Winter Night

(for Pat Dodson)

Though I call across the water no sound rings out
river's escarpments spines of sandstone books
written in a cryptic alphabet
shaped from the movement of twigs in the trees
when I step away from myself
I speak in the voices of night birds
move out from my body into the air above the tide
and hover between the river and night sky
Whose voice comes out of my mouth
never mine when I enter this bay
where I mimic the voice of water fowl
a voice used by the river people
before my grandfather's wooden hull and stroking oars
and my motor and fibreglass
Whose voice returns in a wood-duck's throat
some avenging hunter who shakes
the page of ownership and says we belong
written on rock the old songs
watched as the cliffs crumbled away
the music that rose up from the earth
was the shredded voices of crows
whatever they were called   they walked
differently   with other ways of crying
We came and polished the surface of the river
and holystoned the rock as if it was a deck
chained feathers to breast-plates
filled wings with lice-killing powders
we watched the diamond fire tail finches in clouds
waiting for the seed-eaters to enter their long extinction
with our nets and our guns on our shoulders

Pied Butcher Bird Flute Solo

I steer at full throttle, the boat lifting up
onto the plane, shooting past
Dead Horse Bay, straight under
the bridge and into the upper reaches
of the river. We glide the surface
of the incoming tide, I want to
make it to my marks on time –
now a great white sponge of fog
has come down around us,
it dampens my hair and suddenly
reduces visibility. I cut the motor
and we drift with the tide which takes
the boat close into the shore.
The river narrows and there's eucalyptus
in the atmosphere. Silent now
and almost blind. The fog envelops us.
At first, a few wobbly notes
coming from all sides, a deep throated
fluting climbing the bird-scales,
it loops into a theme, then notes cascade
into a melody that drifts over
the silk of the surface, under the rolling
blanket of fog. So lovely a song
it almost sounds like human-whimsy
becoming a liquid bubbling,
almost a blue yodel, the ghost of Jimmy
Rodgers, then fades again.
A few plopping splashes, mullet
hitting the cotton wool air above them
and landing with belly flops.
We drift silently until a cricket
kicks in with a high, nervous drone
for a thin moment. Almost silence awhile
until that murderous avian spirit
player resumes the masterpiece –
now concert flute, mellow toned
with a sort of back-beat, an amplified pulse
underneath its sweet mock carolling.

Looking into a Bowerbird's Eye

Untamable, fluttering, a feathery
cold pulsing in my hands –
A mature male bowerbird.
House-glow, the night outside,
here the kitchen light reflects
electric splinters, uncountable
shards clustered in a blue eye.
Everything flares to a beak
pecking at fingers, claws
raking the palm of my hand,
alembic depths of blue eye-tissue.
He was trapped in a cupboard at 3 A.M.:
the cat's voice woke the house.
Fingers flecked with specks
of blood now, the eye
a fiery well of indigo cells, cobalt,
ultramarine, cerulean blues.
A pale moon slips through
tree branches outside –
the window pane frames its quarter,
then a squall of refracted
light in eyes that a human
cannot read – opaque, steadfast.
Light sensitive molecules, intricate
lenses, a blue cones of tissue.
Outside, bracing night air – the stars
clustered in the milky way –
my hands, opening, flicked by wings.

The Golden Bird

(for Nathaniel Tarn)

Winter-dusk, darkness closing,
trailing a damp cloak.
Chilling the soft bones of my shoulder's
ingrown wing – pain from
a new wound flickers out –
forking through the rapture of writing,
cold air seeking it.

After reading your book
The Embattled Lyric I feel
closely linked to you – your triple Orpheus,
then Eurydice in all her
changing shapes –
multiple raids on Hades and back
to the light.

Still, these days I prefer
the dark, cold, and a clarity
of mind – even when I feign confusion,
I hold tight to what keeps me
alive – a spur-winged
plover in its broken-wing-dance,
distracting the hawk from her chicks –

Sliding into a trance,
I see the waxing quarter
moon as light across a cotton-wove page –
though now, what act of
imagining could create warmth
from reflected light? Nothing,
silence, blind-air, blank.

Blaise Pascal, testing
a theory, decided finally
to invent a vacuum chamber, a device
that might bring a void into being –
his concept's slug-gun? –
(Like Buckminster Fuller building a tetrahedron
at Black Mountain College.)

At times literary critics mock
poets who imagine
Orpheus harmonising with lyrebirds,
a bird whose song
can pulsate with variations
on a rival's mating call, singing
a kind of bird-jazz.

Today broken words gather
on pages in a broken time,
does the powerful owl's hooting call hang
in some obscure night,
haunting itself? When the last
owl passes, bitter laughter –
the fisher kookaburra, hooking

snakes up from gutters.
Minerva's owl once spread its
wings at dusk and called aloud on our behalf.
W.B. Yeats's final vision
was a gold clockwork bird
to defeat the abyss. When his heart
stopped, did he believe

it would transcend him:
gold-foil wings hovering
over the void, intricate golden beak singing
eternally – after the world's end
beyond hearing? – Ted Berrigan wrote
'I rage in a blue shirt
at a brown desk in a bright room' –

There's a line by Wallace
Stevens, written in a foul
mood on a grey day in Connecticut: 'the sound
of the mind is an echo'. Outside
the window tonight, a star chart
unfolds, on the pane Narcissus inscribes:
The human miracle?

Joseph Cornell's Tools

Joseph Cornell used these sturdy tools
and instruments to create boxes,
time machines. Constructions
made from bits and pieces,
three dimensional frames containing
fans, lace, feathers – other
once ephemeral objects, including
a torn fragment of photography,
an image of Mallarmé's
hands – One contains an illustration
of a humming bird – it seems
to hover in the space between
the glass and the backing of the box.
In another, an etching
of a great horned owl – like the bird
I watched one night,
perched on a light-post in Boulder,
Colorado: it swoops from
memory, filling my study with silent
flight as I recall another
visitation. This afternoon,
returning from the post office
I drove ahead of an approaching storm,
trees shook and a black cockatoo
flew out of them, it sailed on
just ahead of my car for almost a minute,
a long time given the situation –
stroking the air before the windscreen,
following the road, so close
I could see details of its plumage,
two red patches across the tail feathers.
Something other than beautiful, fleeting.

At Rock River

(for Peter O'Leary who drove me to Woodland Pattern, Milwaukee)

In a subway in New York City,
Zukofsky carefully watches

a praying mantis on a page
of newspaper in full defensive

display. In a Milwaukee
factory Niedecker listens to workers

on their lunch-break yarning.
Lines drawn, some in books

others in sand – spinning tangles.
Lorine sorting through

her father's lines that hauled carp.
Everything difficult, even

in hours writing lines of poetry
words came a letter at a time,

creating phrases, images
of buckets tipped over with a light

touch, line breaks making
sense of her sparse life – Rock River's

pull. She changed the water
level until she drew Zuk

and Basil Bunting to her front door.
Green tree frogs croaked

and a barn owl cleared the bone
from its throat. Sound of paddle

splash, then a water rat drops down
from the plank-wood

dock to scurry under netboards.
There was her father's bent back

as he pulled them home
along with the shuddering catch:

carp-scales caught in mesh
were silver coins in broad shafts

of the late sun. Night time,
after the dishes, a dream of hands

roughened on oat-sacks.
Dawn, starling chatter and ratshit,

Lorine watches a white moth
on a stalk of blossoming rose mallow.

After the soft crack of duck eggs –
she sits at her breakfast table, writing

lines including factory talk,
her way, until it seems to matter.

Bolinas Bay, An Ode

(for Joanne Kyger)

At Joanne's, three rainbows over the bay.
In the garden, talking, our birdsong and calls,
spun to metaphors in sunlight –

Words, all afternoon, mingled with
their meanings, songs of light, memories of poets
along sempiternal zones in our heads.

Light, an abstract surf, tides of air behind it
hung with Anna's humming birds:
their condensed flight, the sound of Joanne's

thought – garden trees turned their leaves,
showing veins, pencil-traces of her handwriting
from the 1960s. One day back then

lashing out, she parodied an elder's poem
read it to class – boys in tight with themselves –
her words danced above their heads,

jazz-notes. A moth flutters around a light shade,
leaving traces of silver powder on the globe –
the desire for something afar – I look out

and catch sight of a troupe of blue jays
on a foray into what was left of their day.
Joanne turns in her kitchen, radiating within,

opening her intellect's wings. Memory's atomic
particles collide, sparks glow in Joanne's pupils,
her energies, packing a punch.

Through glass, the first woodpecker I've ever seen,
it slices and chops into a tree trunk
uncovering worms in their cocoons.

Inside Robert Creeley's *Collected Poems*

We learned from *After Mallarmé*, beyond thought's silence there
    was a silence in stone,
a compression of grey language without music, then we began to
    understand difference
between sex in our heads and sex in the bed; the form of women
    a way to hold chaos,
that singing bird, in a cage we imaged you had projected just ahead
    of vision where eyes

remembered a look that killed, our unbelieving bodies listened too
    long to the music
of stone. There were sails waiting in the harbour, oceans beyond
    the beaches and nighthawk moons,
walks along coastlines where the great redwoods stood recording us
    then a loop
in time talking all night with Augustine in Hippo 'a projection of
    the mind'.
All of Africa, in a '67 Mustang down Highway 61 on a river of
    prose as ideas were soaked
by forgotten monsoons as the world blossomed into your voice
    reciting *The Garden*
in a half empty classroom, you recounting afterward yourself as a
    young man
breeding Birmingham Rollers.

The stage without props but shadows with a woman who played
    out the role,
a classic one act show repeating stage directions instead of lines, her
    despairing husband
off stage as a tape-loop, as a wet crow at a cross-road, feathers black
    ink smudging words
in the examinations, your regret bound in so tightly by your lines
    – so it could not leach
away as a guilt pool. We passed those desert mountains and forth
    time round you made
more songs delicate music with flashes of anger stashed for the
    mornings after.

The piled-up manuscripts adrift in kitchens of light your relentless
   questions probing
the ones who loved you, beating your hand and repeating over the
   word 'heart'
until its meaning bruised the hearts that loved. Possible meanings
   returned in *The Finger*,
your tool and your weapon, splitting lines with a ballpoint, tearing
   the flesh the paper,
the page, the personal pronoun stranded then as father to children
   belying kindness
as you'd pad the floor of bedrooms chanting madrigals of fierce love.

No shoes, no issues, no re-writes – and you singing inwardly at the
   door to the gallery,
gliding along through painted skies, the poem taking us into, and
   then out the other side
of the book, laying down lines, word by word on billowing sheets
   waking dreams
three dimensional worlds, alive. The printer setting slugs of type
   your smoke proofs
spelling out the need for a high morale, a way to live the words, yes
   'tell 'em it's fun let's go!'
Although we sit here at the table stunned by time: Creeley's maps
   spread out
across the floor of the tent.

From the hills above Bolinas Bay the turkey vultures hang in the
   clear sky, black handkerchiefs,
parachuting pages – the sky's false Indulgences, while you live on,
   as long as we listen,
and there's no reason to repent.

Summer at Carcoar

(after the painting by Brett Whiteley)

The painter enters   time through the Belubula river,
draws out long bodies   from poplar trees
drenches the air   a Naples yellow hue, polishes water flow
to a waxy sheen   until it sings under glowing light
he turns a bend   a joyous curve and quick line
then moves over   paddocks, back to the place
where he was born   to embrace ideas of chaos, accelerating
particles in his head,   paints original county as a garden
over scars, sketches notes   on the edges, a wren flicks its tail up
and brushstrokes freeze   blue feathers onto surface
the willow pulses salicylic acid   through his idea of pain
the shape of particular hurting   just under skin,
a rock where a currawong   becomes larger than it was
in life, running under   tissues in a burrow where flecks
of the past gleam through   a green subterranean light
from a Hades   of childhood's fears
a crumbling   ground of families,
here we notice   an absence of human figures
and intense deciduous   trees glow
and squat under birdsong   the sun new pain
rabbits hint at movement,   twitch in grasses
details load themselves: golden paddocks
made up in the mind,   river a memory spilling
its ballast   hard discoveries, the ground opened
though intricate   eddies in tides of grass
the ten thousand   brush strokes, branches
of thought   etching themselves under the small sky,
feathers   counted, each leaf a fold
wild   patterns so right you believe the painted world
then   sense an open field believes you   while under ground
around   the boiling core Whiteley's scars
indicate mining,   around 1905 they discovered
uranium here   a local paper called it the parent of radium
we sense in the painting's   glow, stains of undertow
a lash in the black highway   as it curves outside the frame
we too, sense a marsupial instinct   to tunnel down
and glance flowers, mauve bells   ringing their soft trumpets
then a bee's arc describing flight,   a thought becoming amber.

A Visitation

All night, wildfire burned in the tree-tops
on the other side of the river. Now it's morning.
Smoking embers from the angophoras
are landing on the near shore
as a yellow-footed rock wallaby limps, dazed,
from the scrub, its fur matted,
its tail barely able to support its weight.
Although wounded, it seems miraculous:
the soft yellow of its feet, the hard, sharp black
of its claws. It's the first yellow-footer
I've seen for more than forty years. It takes
me back immediately to the time I was a kid,
rowing my grandfather's tallow-wood skiff across
Big Bay: I spotted a mob of four rock wallabies
that stood there as I sat silently in the boat
and let the tide carry me right by them.
One, I noticed, seemed to have mange –
it had mottled fur on its back – like the river foxes
in those days. Then a panic ran through
them: the largest buck bounded, almost flew,
straight up an enormous rock; the sheer wildness
and ferocity of it shocked me. Afterwards,
the atmosphere was thick with an odour unlike
anything I recognised. This morning, it's in the air
again. I turn to take another look, but the
rock wallaby's gone.

The Guard's Advice
(after reading René Char's Les Matinaux*)*

                        An hour before dawn   set down   moths flutter
        from the letterbox   diamond-winged   white-tipped
            fly in circles   around a match flare
our world a match flare   the particular   whiskers
                moth's whiskers trembling   their feathery antennae
receiving what moths   receive   moth talk
                a Parisian radio station   in the background
no news   German takeover talk   back to the grass
        in my region   here now the sun comes
warms my cheeks   even though   just yesterday
                I cursed the heat   then as shadows   lengthened
I thought shadows might be some   kind of protection
        until they became damp   and clung to us
                    shadow-nets   shadow splotches   undergrowth
a fish gasping by a river   the water stained   tea coloured
        a capsized boat   two bodies   and bees
                in the rushes   bees still able   to sting
hanging around too long   for anything   weakens faith
        I waited for her   three months   she was impatient
            for mercy   she wanted to break away
rather than go stale   in the ruins of a school
            a doorstep in the freezing pre-dawn   we made love
a cracked doorstep   wrecked   seating   on canvas
            on my parachute   black silk   white skin   moths
ants moving on   a tracery of snail-slime
            I stay here in my region   our region   she returns
it seemed ridiculous   in the end   she walked
        through the door   in pain   her wound bandaged
            holding an armful of huge dark roses
        she carried their sweet scent   of velvet decay
        her eyes   carrying images
                of the dyker's abusive hands   skins
pale   our faces the pallor of night   fingernails shot
            cracked   then I uncovered   the green apples from
a deserted orchard   fallen fruit   the cold air   biting like a vice
    my knife paring away the bruised flesh
            she carried a message   from a German guard
        whispered it   he said   *whatever else   desert*

Easter Fish

(for Juno Gemes, in memory of her uncle Miklós Radnóti)

Tonight in the bright void of our kitchen, my wife
and her mother cooked dinner and talked of brutal places
at the end of the world and meals scraped together

from remnants: thin brown potato skins, tart green
bean soup. We discussed the rituals of Passover.
Charcoal lines from a recent bushfire cross-hatched

the trunks of ghost gums. Outside our kitchen windows,
a butcher bird appeared on the verandah, strutting
the rail and capriciously fluting.

Later our conversation filled an elegant apartment
in Budapest with music. We spoke – carefully, tenderly
perhaps – of the river, the unbroken Danube.

Our minds can flower suddenly sometimes
with monstrous kelp waving in the tide
flowing from old wounds:

brace yourself, cities of the world, against flood,
famine, invasion. Ruin. Now the river's surface
is stretched tight, marbled by a sun setting

in heads indwelling in silence. Puncturing the sky
upstream, a pair of sea-eagles spiral down to their nest.
We steamed our Good Friday fish,

seasoned with sweet basil and the juice of lemons,
and deliciously the taste brought back memories of its
capture: the mauve and silver flanks fading

into a quick death, the small cold flames of phosphorous
lapping our boat's invisible Plimsoll line, the rising
and falling of our breath.

The Greenshank

Miklós Radnóti, marched from forced labour
in Yugoslavia back into Hungary, came to rest
near a bend in the Radca, at what his translator
describes as 'a strange lonely place' where

the tributary joins 'the great river', a marshland
watched over by willows and 'high circling birds'.
Condors perhaps – they appear in the notes and
poems he was writing – under a foamy sky.

Huddled in a trench with the body of a friend
who'd been shot in the neck, he wrote with a pencil
stub in his notebook: patience flowers into death.
His wife's face bloomed in his head.

Thinking of the petals of crushed flowers
floating in a wake of perfume, he wrote to caress her
neck. The fascists' bullets wipe out his patience.
His written petals survive.

Today, we listen to the news of war
here in a river sanctuary his niece's unbending
will has created – horizontal slats of cedar, verticals
of glass – a Mondrian chapel of light.

This afternoon just before dark the first
greenshank arrived from the Hebrides.
Ignorant of human borders, its migration
technology is simple: feathers

and fish-fuel, cryptic colour and homing
instinct. This elegant wader landed on a mooring,
got ruffled in the westerly, then took off again,
an acrobatic twister, and levelled down

onto a mudflat – a lone figure that dashed across
the shore, stood on one leg, then, conducting
its song with its bill, came forward
in a high-stepping dance.

Black Laughter, Budapest 1934

(after Attila József)

It's summer, it's a fine evening.
The trains rattle through the station,
you can hear the knock-off horns
blaring from the factories,
coal-stained roofs are stained again
by the black night, under
the streetlights the newsboys
yell headlines, cars zip
and skid on the tram-lines
the trams clang one after the other
neon signs flair until you
start to go blind by reading them,
in the back lanes the walls
caked with last week's posters
lean in and stifle your last impulse
to laugh it off – men with
faces straight from cartoons hurry
away from others who want
to hold them back, the necks
of the avenues are stiff with anger.
You can hear the trudging
footsteps of workers heading home
as if they were old mystics
walking to nowhere on this earth.
You can even hear the soft
wrists of pickpockets whispering
between coats, right beside
a man from the country who sighs
as if he's just thrown a stack
of hey onto a cart. I listen to it all,
the beggar who quietly
simpers and wipes his nose,
the woman who looks sideways
for a second or two –
she knows that I'm a stranger here,
so I just sit on a doorstep
and keep my mouth tightly closed.
It's summer, it's a fine evening.

Autumn, Europe 1943

(after Miklós Radnóti)

Seen through steel-coloured clouds, the sun
rises higher and the sky tears itself in two –
a blue flag, a stained shirt cloth.
Poisonous vapours bank up and absorb
the sun's warmth. Below them, we notice
a swallow setting out to leave – we can faintly
hear its call – more like a thin scream.

On the rubble, what's left of the graveyard wall,
a red lizard scuttles. In the air, a live cargo
from autumn's legacy: carnivorous wasps.
On the banked earth, makeshift trenches, men
sit staring at distant fires of death. We can
smell the rot as it settles down through the air.
The dry bracken smoulders, setting free

a swirling eddy of sparks, this flares into flames
from the fiery wind. The coming dark will
illuminate more calligraphy of burning.
In vineyards, grapes shrink to ruined sultanas,
vines wither and their dry yellow flowers
crackle in wind, dropping seeds onto
the burning ground. Whole fields are beginning

to sink into this sea of smoke and mist.
We hear an insane clattering of huge carts
that shake what's left of the leaves off the branches
of ancient trees. Look my love, there
in your hair, a golden leaf, fallen from a branch
shaking above your head. Everything's starting a drift
into exhausted sleep, but wait, look

there's death, finally lovely in its glide down
the valley as the sky cradles what's left of the garden.
One last wise move, together, let's love each
other then lean into sleep. Out there, the thrush
has been asleep for a while, kiss me now, fall with me.
The walnuts fall onto the piles of dead leaves
without making a sound. And reason falls apart.

Black Laughter, Sydney

It was twilight in a rowing boat on Sydney Harbour.
Out from Blues Point, I was pulling hard
on the oars of a hired rowboat to be
returned before the natural curfew of darkness –
this was over thirty years ago and memories
are complex things – one image is stronger
than the others, flying foxes moving in black files
across the sky above the harbour, flying
out from my childhood into their present
continuing for a million years or so.
This memory comes back each time my resolve
to keep my soul free from stain weakens,
even for a moment: the bats, the determined
pulling on the oars. A westerly wind
was chopping up the harbour, wakes from
ferries slapped against the wooden skiff,
I was wet to the skin and bailing out with a can.
When I made it to the Quay I found
myself walking through a crowd of people
who were smartly dressed and eating cold canapés.
It was a reception for a triple marriage,
three brides and their grooms married under
the sails of the Opera House, there were comments
about real estate and flying fish. On the corner
of the street a busker swung a bullroarer
and handed round a hat, two cops in a V8 car
parked at the kerb revved up the motor in time
to the homeless man's blunt instrument.
A woman explained this whole event
had been hexed by some witch in King's Cross –
a pigeon fancier offered news that predators
lived high in the city's glass canyons – each night
raptors swooped to kill the road-peckers,
along with racing birds still homing though the dusk.
It was twilight in a rowing boat on Sydney Harbour.

The Intervention

(for Ali Cobby Eckerman)

When Yeats writes, *Soul clap its hands*
and sing, and louder sing, it feels tangible,
and yet a friend says we can't use
the word 'soul' these days, but
then adds, all the more reason. When
I heard you reading your poetry
in Castlemaine, a long steady song,
I was breathing the air of your soul,
we were both hundreds of miles from
our own countries, your body swayed
as you called up a whole world,
with images and stories woven
through with suffering. Lines
were licks of lightning, some thin
as the chill of your meanings that
we all recognised – all I can compare
this with is the feeling you get
swimming alongside a shark, or
the shot of joy in watching a lyrebird
shaking out its tail in full display,
pouring all song into its own singing.

Praise and Its Shadow

Standing on this rocky shore
at the end of the point, sun's
hitting sandstone escarpments as it sinks,
colouring everything red –
I watch the felty black surface
of the river carrying pelicans
downstream to the mouth.
I could easily disappear into
this landscape, become
a fisherman again and work
the tide through the moon's cycles
and its darks, pierced with stars –
A local Novalis, courting
the night itself – my nets always
coming in without a catch,
at dawn each new day my head full
of emptiness, nothing there
but love for the long, echoing darkness.

Death of a Cat

Siamese seal-pointer, ghost cat.
My familiar and killer,
sleeper under covers.
A true carnivore
devoured hundreds of pilchards
maybe thousands,
and many baby brown snakes.

That pair of kingfisher bodies.
First the pale female,
jumped and tortured.
Then the male
who returned to help his mate
and met death by tooth and claw.

Roller of lizards and skinks,
blue-eyed and sleek.

Bully-boy with a foul tongue,
most articulate at night.
Shiny, cream-furred cuddler,
brown-eared stalker.
Attention seeker and bird watcher.
My wife's tormentor.

The one who ate a dozen
live garfish whole,
stolen from the bait-tank.
Taut-bodied, razor-footed climber
with sprung-rhythm.
Stuck among branches yowling.

Ripping the chairs apart,
while purring for praise.
A 'legend' according to my son,
to my wife, a demented prowling beast.

My darling and terrible
King Tut, who prowled here
for eighteen years, before The Mower
cut out his kidneys.

PART TWO

Eurydice and the Mudlark

Sunlight fades the coloured spine
of *What Bird Is That?* The shadow

of your hand marks my face:
wings and the tips of fingers,

coiled hands in the tiny egg
or sac of living tissue,

dredge up a likeness beyond
appearance. Morning unfurls,

I wake and shave. In the mirror
the reflection of a mudlark's tail-fan

echoes the silence of glass.
We hover all day on the surface

of the stream, above a soft bottom,
until moonlight falls again

onto stark white bed-sheets.
The shadow your hand casts

resembles the mudlark, opening
its wings, calling and rocking,

perched in the pages
of my book.

Letter to Eurydice

Watercolour moon, the window-panes
fogged up. Outside, the river

slips by; an overhanging blackbutt
branch inscribes the surface

with a line across foaming run-off.
Living near mudflats I'm protected

by mangroves: in winter
the southerly rakes their curly heads,

the green skirts are my windbreak.
At the Fork these summer thoughts

are silted up and become obscure:
it's more than halfway into a big ebb

and my mind's a dark moat. If you
get this far – *watch it* – and step

on my dreams, you'll find
they've been pulped. It's only flight

that matters here; take a break and fling
your next thought onto the tide.

In these parts, the lyrebird must carry
its own cage on its back

through swamps – I once believed this.
But yesterday the bird suffered a stroke.

'It keeps falling to the ground,' the ranger
said, 'nothing can be done.' It's time

to commiserate with this creature,
all songbird but not quite lyre.

The Floating Head

I turned off electricity, pulled telephone cords
out of the wall, saw stars in glass through cedar slats.
I wrapped a scarf around my headache
and looked inside –

an ebbing memory leaving with the tide.
My boat's motor roared and I hurtled across
the river into blazing cold night
then circled back.

Crouched in a corner of the house,
my cat borrows my voice – I talk
to him through the night. The heater
clicks, its pilot light blinks. I scribble

a few lines, pass my fishing rod off
as a lyre. Who needs this bitter tune?
Its distorted chords lull me into numbness.
I bend it over double and pluck.

The Serpent

Twenty crows gathered on a branch,
bare in the early summer's heat.
We strung a bow from the willow tree

and used bamboo for arrows.
The afternoon thrummed with locusts.
Clouds at the end of the sky

were alive with the thunder that shook
the corrugated iron. We were wet
with sweat – it was a hundred degrees

that day, Granny said, hot as blood Hades.
It was Christmas time – the girls
were up for holidays – and we were

playing under the verandah. The sun
spread a golden glow in the calm
before the gathering storm

as the first snake of the season
came slithering out of the fowl yard,
leaving us its red-checked skin

Eurydice and the Tawny Frogmouth

On the low arch
above our gate,
he looks out
through a fringe
of feathers,
hunting,
then places one
foot on black
cast iron and ruffles
his head. His other
foot is clenched
in the night air,
held out
in an atmosphere
of waiting – then
unclenched.
Those nights
flying with you
weighed no more
or less than
this.

Singing His Head Off

He stumbles on a rocking pontoon
at the end of his long wharf,
tying things down – greasy ropes

loop around pylons, old tires hang
from boats. He was ferryman
at Kangaroo Point before the bridge

was built and his horse and punt
decommissioned – it's all gone
into myth now. His arms almost float

in the humid air, he's barely there.
He coalesces around the feeling of loss
of his wife in his stomach.

She's been underground for a week.
He invited no one to the funeral
and has given up speaking.

Cockatoos in the tall melaleucas
above the graveyard drop seed husks
and shake their sulfur crests.

Standing now with his back to the storm,
he straightens and begins to sing –
a deep low moan building

to a howl and a high elemental
keening – his song that could once
make rocks weep.

Eurydice, after a Midnight Storm

A koel glides from a nest
abandoned by owls.
We wade in a tide
of humidity. Blue
morning-glory vines
grow in thick night,
undergrowth's stranglers.
The storm breaks
and moves out to sea.
I smell you in the calm
air, an edgy presence,
as house lights
blink on one by one
and Easter's garbled noise
is switched off, then walk
to the edge of the river
and listen to the tide
rush downstream.

Eurydice in Sydney

What was he thinking while I was gone?
Was his mind still doing time in his head,
dancing in abstract darkness?

Pain comes and goes. I notice things
I hadn't before: the city ibis stitching its voice
to the wind between car park and George Street.

I think of going shopping with him.
Bogong moths in a shaft of sunlight
flutter beneath the blue trees

of a shadowy Hyde Park. Does
Sydney Harbour still exist? Depends
on how his voice murmurs

late into night as he drinks, rustling
still with that old ardour, trailing ribbons
of smoke and blood.

Eurydice Combs Her Hair

We reach the end of a bay
and cut in through mangroves.
Our boat hits the bottom,
kicks up mud and sand.
Crossing a deep hole,
the water changes texture –
the surface becomes choppy –
and the trees along the shore here
are the colour of salmon fillets.
A whipbird cracks its call
down a sandstone escarpment
as we anchor up and the sun
sets behind clouds. I sing to you,
wherever you are. In the dark's
chill I can smell your hair,
even though you're
beyond reach.

Eurydice Agape

A preacher came to Calabash Creek
in an expensive four-wheel drive.
He set up in the little park
with his team of technicians.
Bose speakers hung from the gum trees.
The kookaburras started laughing
just before dark.

An oyster farmer's punt, full of
drunks from the Workers Club,
took off from the mudflats and roared
into the night. They called us a bunch
of cunts. Before long the children
from the point were speaking
in tongues. The singing

was fabulous – a woman sang
the Statesboro Blues – and there
was talk of miracles. Then the
preacher spoke of Hell. Suddenly
my arms were full, you started
sobbing, my face was wet with tears.
You were back in paradise.

Eurydice on Fire

A shapeless field of mist above the river's
surface, drifting. At first light the head

of a tree emerges, then black sticks
from oyster racks. The mist

parts as it rolls across
a channel pole's yellow marker –

another level of watching settles
in thinking the mist

forms ribbons and leaves
wisps of itself

in mangrove branches.
My head starts burning,

jagging its hurt deeply: here's
a woman caught in time,

unable to grow old.
She's never said a word

I've heard of. Can she speak?
Do I have any choice?

I step clear, fully alight,
for long enough to think

What's to say? Her voice
echoes the absence.

Eurydice Reads *Roots and Branches*

Torchlight flares on the book's
cover – reading's difficult in the boat –
and you wonder, is the helmsman
distracted by light?
                                On this river
there's only one destination, that dock
on the other side. The pages
are smeared by yellow light-beams:
    What time of day is it?
                        What day of the month?
    We continued the crossing – flowering gums,
bees flying by polarised light – then watched
a shape forming, an emerald blur of wings
at the periphery of torchlight, a bee-eater
hovering over words, over the hive
of the book.
                      We taste honey
on our tongues – an orange beak flashes –
and read to one another in pitch dark,
carried on the wings of words.

Thinking of Eurydice at Midnight

My Siamese cat's left a brown
snake, its back broken, on my desk.
The underground throbs outside my window.
The black highway of the river's crinkled by a light
westerly blowing down. I want to give praise
to the coming winter, but problems
of belief flare and buckle under
the lumpy syntax. The unelected
President's on the radio again,
laying waste to the world.

Faith – that old lie. I drag up
impossible meanings and double divisions
of love and betrayal, light and dark.
Where on earth am I after all these years?
A possum eats crusts on the verandah,
standing up on its hind legs.
My weakness can't be measured.
My head contains thousands of images –
slimy mackerel splashing about in the murk.
My failures slip through fingers pointed
at the best night of my life. This one.

The cold mist falls, my head floats in a stream
of thinking. Eurydice. Did I fumble? Maybe
I was meant to be the moon's reflection
and sing darkness like the nightjar. Why
wouldn't I infest this place, where the
sun shines on settlers and their heirs
and these heirlooms I weave
from their blond silk?

PART THREE

The Flag-tailed Bird of Paradise

(George W. Bush instructed 'the enemy' to hold up
white flags and stand twenty metres away from their tanks,
promising that if they did, they would be spared.)

Thought to be extinct, they are appearing
through the red mist, their white tails

waving at blunt helicopters
splattering the earth. These creatures

from paradise play dead when attacked:
they freeze, clamped to a branch, the tiny

flags on their tails barely shimmering in
broken sunlight. They once lived

in jungles on islands in the Pacific,
but haven't been found dead there

since 1958. Some escaped to Arabia:
sold to collectors and bred in captivity,

they were taken up by zoos, kept in palaces
and inbred. Flunkies fed them and sultans

hovered about them, marvelling at how
they became extraordinary in their

deformities – their cream-coloured plumage
shot through with pale, beautiful rainbows,

their eyes enormous, pink, and their
flag-tails heavy – almost too heavy

to hold up, but not theirs
to withhold.

The Goldfinches of Baghdad

These finches are kept in gold cages
or boxes covered in wire mesh;
they are used by falcon trainers as lures,
and rich patriarchs choose these living ornaments
to sing to them on their deathbeds. Their song is pure
and melodious. A goldfinch with a slashed throat
was the subject of a masterpiece painted in the
sixteenth century on the back of a highly
polished mother-of-pearl shell – it burns
tonight in Baghdad, along with the living,
caged birds. Flesh and feathers, hands
and wings. Sirens wail, but the tongues
of poets and the beaks of goldfinches burn.
Those who cannot speak burn along with the
articulate – creatures oblivious of prayer burn
along with those who lament to their god.
Falcons on the silver chains, the children
of the falson trainer, smother in the smoke
of burning feathers and human flesh.
We sing or die, singing death
as our songs feed the flames.

The Stone Curlew

I am writing this inside the head
of a bush stone curlew,
we have been travelling for days

moving over the earth
flying when necessary.
I am not the bird itself, only its passenger

looking through its eyes.
The world rocks slightly as we move
over the stubble grass of the dunes,

at night shooting stars draw lines
across the velvet dark
as I hang in a sling of light

between the bird's nocturnal eyes.
The heavens make sense, seeing this way
makes me want to believe

words have meanings,
that Australia is no longer a wound
in the side of the earth.

I think of the white settlers
who compared the curlew's song
to the cries of women being strangled,

and remember the poets who wrote
anthropomorphically as I sing softly
from the jelly of the stone curlew's brain.

The Jesus Bird

The lotus-bird's signature
is slenderness, moving

without ring-marking water's
skin-tight surface.

A colourist, strokes tone
with a wing, fans out pinions:

The show's to escape
death in shape of harrier

or swamp's light-slashing pike.
The night watch is a dance

where bird antenna
probes mind-stepping illusions

to parry with a stray
plug-throwing fisherman,

alert in thin air
whirred by a dragonfly's

cellophane propeller,
or puttering swamp-bugs.

When the creek's back is dark
glass, a conjure, striper,

lotus-dancing with river-pimps.
Creek alley's sideshow.

The Great Knot

Alterant birds, alterant words
and Bunting's descant on a madrigal,
Zukofsky's 'descrying black-hellebore

white white double flowered
marshmallow mallow-rose
snowstorm sea-hollyhock'

and you're dancing with words in particular.
This bird's a traveller, summers
in north-eastern Siberia,

winters in southern China
and has vagrants that fly to Australia.
Zukofsky's flowers are words in bloom

strung out along the song lines,
the great knot as tricky as whisky
running along whisky-coloured shores

where clear water laps granite
and salt water foams on the sandstone.
Its shadow shoots over lagoons

rancid with verbiage in disintegration
as it tries to describe the sink ponds of paper mills,
factories discharging, alterant poems.

The Southern Skua

The skua flew into our heads in 1968 –
a new kind of poetry, a scavenging predator
frequently attacking humans,
flying through the streets of seaside towns,
foraging with seagulls. This bird
has few predators. One was found
in Tasmania, its beak embedded in the skull
of a spotted quoll, dragged
into a clearing by devils. They form clubs
and proclaim their territory
by various displays and loud aggressive calls;
they are agile metaphysicians,
sweeping along lines of projective verse,
echoing each other's songs.
Although the skua breeds on Black Mountain
it is migratory and dispersive, its call
a series of low quacks and thin whinnying squeals.
They are omnivorous and critical creatures;
animal liberationists never mention
the habits of skua. If you read skua poetry, beware:
one could fly out from the page
and change the expression on your face.

The Pheasant-tailed Jacana

The canoe wings its way upstream.
A school of garfish scatter
around lily-pads, streaking

silver pencils, scribbling nonsense;
their gut-sacks translucent,
alive with insect larvae, calligraphic ink.

Green and difficult, wet
feathers trailing, the jacana draws
lines of cobweb through sunlight

picking off spinning dragonflies;
air bubbles rise from the mouth
of a lungfish under its surface stepping feet.

Maybe an image of the jacana
comes to the insane remembering Jesus.
Up here in the jungle

we see flowers glowing,
smelling as sweet in the fist of a drunk,
stumped for meaning, grumbling

back at his own face reflected
on a flowing sheet of the creek's surface.
Leaping back into the picture, stepping out

with its long tail held high
for no reason but instinct, its eyes drawing in
shapes we cannot know.

Arctic Jaeger

This bird comes between the light
and your reading, hang-glides
in a corner of your eye, a pirate

with a feather in its cap – a sly con
riding the breath of your best line;
flying straight out of Olson's delirium tremens

hangs around with dead fish
under its wing; heavier than a night heron
like a loose-winged falcon:

take its shape to mean blood sport
on our terms. Lines drawn from the breath,
one flash of meaning following

another, a bad draft in its claw
a quote from Cohen's *The Future*
in its bill – this bird cuts out descriptions,

its flight over bleak oceans
tells no story, its white plumage a flying page
written in a language not endangered.

The Cow Bird

This is not poetry – this bird's turkey-head
has a craw that produces crap – its chicks,
        feeding, get covered in a stench
        you could compare

to the breath of an alcoholic cane toad
that's feasted on a bucket of rancid pork.
        The descriptive drift
        throws up this internationalist:

the hoatzin (pronounced *what-seen*),
lives on the banks of the Orinoco River
        flowing through the central
        plains of Venezuela.

Young hoatzins dive-bomb the surface
from their nests overhead, swim
        underwater then pull themselves
        back up into the trees

with their clawed wing-tips.
The idea of these creatures has been known
        to drive scientific investigators
        crazy: infesting the imaginations

of phytochemists from within,
they create themselves from the dark
        whims of their hosts, parachuting
        in through their eyes.

Good students have fried their brains
contemplating the mating habits
        of the cowbird – they are, however, pure
        joy to confessional poets,

who weave them in as tropes as they write poems
concerning their wedding night, in which they
        consummate their bliss oozing
        the milk of what-seens.

The Hudsonian Godwit

Although it breeds in Hudson Bay,
it winters in South America.
However, a lone vagrant godwit
was found at Kooragang Island
in New South Wales before
the Christmas of 1982 – word
spread quickly and many observers
travelled to Newcastle to see it.
They are still searching. This
Australian godwit's call – *toy, toy, toy* –
was recorded and this recording
has been compared to the work
of Phil Spector. Its markings are
complex and beautiful, with
prominent white supercilium,
dorsum deep grey with each feather
fringed white, its underparts mainly
soot-grey. It is a bird for objectivists.
It wades through the shallows,
its bill making rapid stitching motions
as it sews together its own wake.
The godwit's cryptic markings
make it a perfect object for the similes
of Australia's 'greatest imagist' –
but don't look, you won't find it.

Red-necked Avocet

Wading in a lake, its entrance
to the sea blocked, our legs
illuminated by white-hot
mantles burning kerosene
in pressure lamps, it was all
detail. Could we know
the avocets were victims?
The acid from our joint
imagination billowed
behind us, a killing wake:
we were all eyes. Huge prawns
kicked up under our toes,
then zapped away into weeds;
the wings of black swans fanned
our desire to eat the avocet's
fragile, mottled eggs. We tried
to feed one of the chicks
boiled prawns; she looked
angelic as she shuddered.
The fire on the sand crackled
with dead bulrush canes and spat
whizzing, popcorn-sized embers;
flames licked the black
of the moon. Our cotton clothes
soaked up the smoke's breath.
We were drunk with salt
and sand, with killing, eating
prawns, talking rubbish, having
fun. Avocets migrated from our
thoughts into sound as they
too became human.

Major Mitchell's Pink Cockatoo

In the Mallee, dodging crooked branches of mulga
trees, she waits like a sundial for our caravan,
her clear voice a distinct falsetto attracting
passion police and painted quail. Time the cracker
keeps her harmful – her sweat's a fixative, printing alluring
shadows on skin, sketches intricate with pain. We track her
by the dark tan wickerwork winds make of her nests.
The world crumbles into red sand as she takes
my place – neither bird nor feathered tease
of her flock – and I walk out, prepared to let fall –
look – my frame, tail-shaped, fanning air.
Getting nowhere.

Eclectus Parrot

Bright green, scarlet-bellied, black-billed bird
crash lands in campsite. Fire burns cub's fingers.
The scoutmaster flicks the billy with a switch
and growls. Smoke billows and turns brown.

This picture-on-a-biscuit-tin is being
painted as we read: the politician as artist
on his weekend fishing trip. His son,
an eagle scout, hammers the billy

with a triangle. Now hundreds
of budgerigars wheel across a low sky:
the whole jumble's put together from used
landscapes garnished with raptors.

The Minister of Defence has news for these
creatures. He mimics the eclectus parrot –
his face turns red like its satin belly – but his
black beak's genetically engineered for speech.

Gang-gang Cockatoos

In the outer suburbs we pass under them,
dark grey with white stripes, in swishing
fractals of tropical vegetation,
screeching metal songs,

swinging upside down, juggling
pine-nuts – very funny but beyond us.
My state of mind's stencilled on the
footpath, my footprints identical

to gang-gangs': there's a crevice in my
forehead, with a slash of grey, but overall my
head's a red hood. As for my tremulous
tone of voice, who'd believe such

flickering convictions? I smile because
things are so pleasant here: my lightweight
cotton top's cool on humid days, and the
southerly each afternoon

ruffles my feathers, so that sometimes
I chuckle. Since my children left New
York and set up house in exclusive
suburbs – well? The colossal

phone bills, the visits maybe once
in three years, snaps of the kids dressed
as gang-gang chicks in a delightful garden,
the daughter-in-law pecking for money,

private schools to teach them 'Hello Cocky'
– it's 'swell'. I've never used that word,
just wanted to indicate I'm familiar
with the tone used in the cages

of middle America. Gang-gang women
know the score and take it on the chin:
we scorn the first person singular because
at night we drift beyond it.

The Ruff

It's difficult to describe the ruff.
This bird's a live metaphor, puffing
its plumage into simile. A rough
attempt at meaning: though a
waterbird, it dances onshore.

Its colours? Sepia, cream, and
specks of red. These tones bleed well
for watercolourists, but a cock ruff
in display looks top-heavy, often
toppling over into absurdity or worse.

Ruff's a word from the sixteenth century:
feathers goffered into ornaments
for sex. Ritual is human. These cock
birds blow up by instinct, strutting
as if to get across how inhuman

they are, how utterly bird. They
dance in lines of ruff music; some
have suggested that a feather's cadence,
once heard, conducts this dance –
a puffed pose, its head hidden by dark

cowling and the eyes blinded by display.
The ruff's ways delight us if we have
a sense of humour or a dash of
madness: the way of the ruff
is for folk who take themselves

seriously, for this bird's habits
contradict words, art, and human
silence. A ruff occurs at the fringes
of things, in the gap between it
and words. Ruff.

The Grey Whistler

There's a man knocking at the door.
He was a friend once; these days
he's on his last legs – body and soul

stitched together by the court of petty
sessions, he makes a living serving writs.
Samples of deliverance are considered

by the jurists, so I provide details
of my shame – by drawing, for example,
a tropical whistler. Once called the brown

whistler, it lives in mangrove swamps
and their adjoining rainforests. This bird
creates hatches in dense foliage: you can

reach into them and salvage a shabby
pillow of whistler-down created by
tropical humidity, as soft as the texture

of human sorrow. Our friend's ex-wife
was a model who pranced the catwalks
in gowns embroidered with luminous

flecks from the whistler's pinions –
the handiwork of that one-eyed Italian
who made his name in Paris. I have some

fabric in a basket – let's turn it into a hood.
Next time he knocks, I'll pull it over my
head and act dumb. Peggy, there's a good

girl, stay calm – I'm a husk each time
you wince. But the knocking at the door
continues. In the backyard lemon tree,

there's a city crow coughing its lungs up.
As the night goes on, the man outside
becomes the Grey Whistler.

The Dollarbird

As the family listened to the reading
of the will, dollarbirds were landing,
summer migrants thudding into soft
magnolia trees in bloom. It seems
I'll be able to free this captive life
of my mind, let it fall from my eyes
like fish scales and just walk away –
now she'll be okay financially at least.

My conscience, the bully, keeps honing
these blunt threats daily. How much
freedom will she take, how many lozenges
of grief in brown paper bags? I'll scatter
rotten fruit on the terrace and every flying
insect on the northern peninsula will loop
and scuttle in droves for the feast. Dollarbirds

will hawk for them in the air. Translucent,
she glides through my thoughts reading
The Divine Comedy in the compartment
I've filed her in. Bad? Sure, but there's more
housework to be done in my head today.
Pawpaws rot efficiently – they attract pests
from miles away, hovering and crawling.

As she listens, her cheeks glow, her thoughts
swerve as elegantly as dollarbirds, gathering
the words to strike. There's a cavil, a hiccup
and a shudder down her spine. Thirty years
of gibberish, resentments drenched in perfume,
years of love and an inkling she could be wrong.

Can I siphon off the fertilising fantasy and let
passion wither like old skin? Unpleasant
metaphors vanish, migrate back to where
those green-feathered beakies come from:
a dollarbird tumbles as it flies above
magnolia trees in bloom.

The Red-bearded Bee-eater

The swinging gate to the resort
was a rickety affair, its hinges
sang to the ratchet-throated bower birds.
The atmosphere was a thousand years
thick as I pushed through
the crumbling day: then green
wings opened and I was away –
The surf thumped against a beach,
children scrambled in a nearby park
pulling strings controlling
a huge rice-paper bird flapping
along the grass. A man in a monk's
habit walked out of the bush
handed me a pair of gloves
with orders to pull weeds.
Sure I'm having a drink now, it's
already dark but no oblivion –
there's a burning hell in my head,
and I can't make out the birds
from fruit bats in this paradise
of palm trees. Finally my wife
and children carried me
to our quarters – I woke at dawn,
feeling alive I walked about,
I opened the bathroom cupboard,
there was a bare wall at its back
and in the plaster a red-bearded bee-eater
had drilled a hollow for its nest:
inside two chicks rolled their big heads
and squawked for bees.

Rainbow Bee-Eaters
(for my Juno-bird)

Their wings fuelled
by a knowledge of bees,

turning on axles of air,
each crescent beak

an orange-coloured talisman
Once snowy-headed elders

gathered honey bags
in turpentine forests

feathery blurs eating bees
hovering miracles

alongside ancient cliffs
flashed brightly

Your film exposed to them
transparencies

to stay love by catching day
light on pages

the translucent calligraphy
of wings

Lyrebirds

I went back to see the house I rented
during my factory days. It was here
I saved money for my first
typewriter. The factories have closed
or moved away, except one – a sinister
red-brick building, windowless,
without signs – yet in front, a pole
flying the Australian flag.
I parked and listened to the muffled
sounds of light industry,
then watched the workers file out
after their shifts, the younger
men loitering around a parking lot.
Some looked like the old gang,
ruthless delinquents. I beckoned
and one of them walked up to my car.
I asked what happened inside
and he replied, 'First, we attach copper-wings,
then spot-weld aluminium scrolls
for the tails, we don't muck about,
there's money in lyrebirds these days.'

Double-eyed Fig Parrot

A camellia-scented breeze
parts the shore and bruises the apple I'm eating. My free will
drifts across the river. It's been raining and silver
gulls feast on the sepia run-off.

I've been up all night
in the boat-shed painting my year-long affair with abstraction.
Now I try to write but words stick to my fingers
above the screen's blind abyss. So I draw instead, with
charcoal on creamy paper: half-formed wings
of teal appear, sketches of talons and beaks. Actual
wings part the air outside and a possum's knocking
simulates a jazz beat on the roof.

One winter morning,
a dealer arrives with a truckload of caged birds. I feast my eyes,
exotic, on the delicate colours of a double-eyed fig parrot.
Have I ever seen one of these creatures before? I make
a few phone calls, discover that no one knows
who I've become. My family suggests a travel cure.

The plane arrives at Perth –
change that to London – in a smudged dawn. I catch a cab to
the nearest hotel in a mood that fogs the light of my room.
When I open the luggage, it contains only a stub
of charcoal, and hundreds of drawings of a single bird,
all the same specimen: a double-eyed
fig parrot.